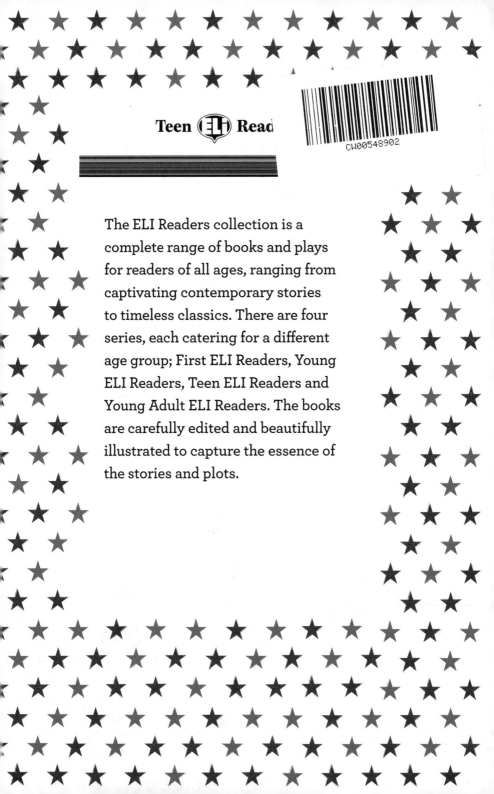

Teen (ELI) Read

CW00548902

The ELI Readers collection is a
complete range of books and plays
for readers of all ages, ranging from
captivating contemporary stories
to timeless classics. There are four
series, each catering for a different
age group; First ELI Readers, Young
ELI Readers, Teen ELI Readers and
Young Adult ELI Readers. The books
are carefully edited and beautifully
illustrated to capture the essence of
the stories and plots.

Flag of Honor

This flag is created from the names of those who perished in the terrorist attacks of September 11, 2001 and February 26, 1993
Now and forever it represents their immortality
We shall never forget them

The FSC® certification guarantees that the paper used in these publications comes from certified forests, promoting responsible forestry management worldwide.

For this series of ELI graded readers, we have planted 5000 new trees.

Angela Tomkinson

Enjoy
New York

Illustrated by
Simone Massoni

Teen ELI Readers

Enjoy New York
by Angela Tomkinson
Language Level Consultant: Lisa Suett
Illustrated by Simone Massoni

ELI Readers
Founder and Series Editors
Paola Accattoli, Grazia Ancillani, Daniele Garbuglia (Art Director)

Graphic Design
Airone Comunicazione - Sergio Elisei

Layout
Airone Comunicazione - Enea Ciccarelli

Production Manager
Francesco Capitano

Photo credits
Shutterstock, Grazia Ancillani

New edition 2021
First edition 2016
© ELI s.r.l.
P.O. Box 6
62019 Recanati MC
Italy
T +39 071750701
F +39 071977851
info@elionline.com
www.elionline.com

Typeset in 13 / 18 pt Monotype Dante
Printed in Italy by Tecnostampa - Pigini Group Printing Division - Loreto Trevi – ERT 244..10
ISBN 978-88-536-3201-2

www.eligradedreaders.com

Contents

These icons indicate the parts of the text that are recorded

start   **stop** ▇

Areas

A

2 New York is a very big city and about 8.4 million people live there. So where do all these people live and work in New York? Let's read about the five areas which are called 'boroughs' or 'districts'.

Queens

In this borough you can visit the Queens Museum of Science, the Billie Jean King National Tennis Center, Socrates Sculpture Park, the Queens Botanical Gardens and The American Museum of the Moving Image. In 1939 the World Fair was here, in Flushing Meadows, which is now the home of the US Open Tennis Championships.

Did you know...?

In Queens you can visit Louis Armstrong's house. He was a jazz musician and played the trumpet*.

The Bronx

This is the place where hip hop was born. It's also home to the New York Yankees and you can watch their baseball matches in the Yankee Stadium.

Do you like playing or watching golf? Here, there's the Van Cortlandt golf course. It was built in 1895 and it's America's oldest golf course.

Did you know...?

You can visit the home of the American writer Edgar Allan Poe in the Bronx. He went to live at Poe Cottage in 1846 and wrote some of his most famous works there.

trumpet:
a ride:
sights: important things to see in a city
film director: a person who makes films

Brooklyn

You can arrive in Brooklyn by walking across the amazing Brooklyn Bridge. Here you can find the area called *DUMBO (Down Under the Manhattan Bridge Overpass)*. It's an important area for art and food. If you want to enjoy yourself in Brooklyn, then why not visit the Brooklyn Children's Museum or go to Coney Island to see the New York Aquarium or go on a ride⋆ at the Coney Island Luna Park?

Did you know...?

Two important sports stars were born in Brooklyn – the boxer Mike Tyson and the basketball player Michael Jordan!

Staten Island

You can get there by going across one of four bridges, or taking the boat from Manhattan. We can often see Staten island in American films or TV series. In fact, some of the parts of *War of the Worlds, The Astronaut's Wife, A Beautiful Mind* and *The Godfather* were made there.

Did you know...?

Staten Island is also the home of tennis. The first American National Tennis Championship was played there in 1880.

Manhattan

Manhattan is divided into three parts – Downtown, Midtown and Uptown. More people live in Manhattan than in the other four boroughs and many tourists visit this area. Here we can find many famous museums and sights⋆ like the Museum of Modern Art, the Metropolitan Museum of Art, the Empire State Building, Wall Street, Times Square and Broadway.

Did you know...?

The American film director⋆ Woody Allen made a film called *Manhattan* in 1979.

Buildings

B

▶ 3 **In New York you can find all kinds of buildings. Tall buildings, small buildings, old buildings, new buildings, beautiful buildings, ugly buildings... So many buildings!**

Empire State Building

In New York there are about 5,845 skyscrapers*. One of these is the Empire State Building. It's on the famous 5th Avenue in Manhattan. It takes its name from one of the nicknames* of New York – the Empire State.

When it was built in 1931, it was the world's tallest building for almost 40 years and it's now America's fourth tallest building. It has 102 floors and from the top you can see a wonderful view of New York.

Flatiron Building

This unusual building was built in 1902 and at that time it was one of the tallest buildings in New York. The people of New York thought that when it was windy, the building would fall down. It's a symbol* of New York and in 1989 it became a 'National Historic Landmark*'.

One World Trade Center

This building was built where the World Trade Center stood until September 11th 2001.
It stands at 541.3 meters and it's the fourth tallest building in the world. It was built in 2006 and finally opened on November 1st 2014. It has 104 floors and at the top there is the One World Observatory where you can see amazing views of New York.

skyscraper: a very tall building
nickname: when people give you an informal name
symbol: (here) when people think of this building, they think of New York
National Historic Landmark: a title given to places of historical importance

New York's narrowest building

You can find this little house at 75½ Bedford Street in Greenwich Village. It's only 3 meters wide and some very famous people have lived there, such as the actor Cary Grant. In August 2013 someone bought the house for $3.25 million.

New York's oldest building

This very old building was built in 1652 and it's the oldest building in New York. It's in Brooklyn and was built by Dutch immigrants who came to live in the city. Now it's a museum where you can learn about life in the past and what it was like to live there.

'Fake' buildings

On the outside you could think that it's a normal house but behind the front wall there are no rooms or a family living there. Near the house there's the subway and behind it there's a tunnel that people can use if something goes wrong on the subway.

Did you know...?
New York is home to the United Nations. Its building is in Manhattan near the East River and has been there since 1952.

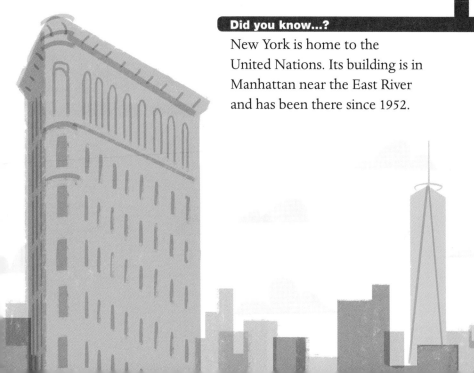

Culture

C

4 **If you like art, museums, street art or other kinds of culture, then you'll find it all here in New York. Let's go on a cultural tour of the city!**

Art and museums

In New York there are some of the most famous and most important art museums in the world! Inside The Metropolitan Museum of Art (The Met) you can find works of art from every part of the world, paintings and sculptures★ from important painters and modern art. The Museum of Modern Art (MoMA) exhibits very important works of art from artists such as Cézanne, Van Gogh, Gauguin, Picasso, Rousseau, Matisse. The Guggenheim Museum was designed by Frank Lloyd Wright and it hosts special exhibitions of modern and contemporary art.

Do you know...?

One of New York's smallest museums is Mmuseumm. It is full of unusual objects, such as a shoe that somebody threw at the US President in 2008, and it is built inside a lift!

Do you know...?

In New York there's even a skyscraper museum! It isn't inside a skyscraper but it's related to skyscrapers.

 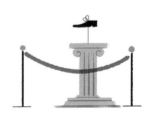

sculpture:

secret: something that you don't tell anyone about

setting: the time and place of a film/book

Street art

If you like street art, then it's possible to go on a walking tour of the areas in the city that have walls and buildings full of graffiti and art. But it isn't possible to see all the street art in the city! In 2009 a group of 100 street artists started the Underbelly Project. They painted for one night each in an old subway station that wasn't used anymore. It was a secret* and not many people knew about it. Now the entrance to the subway station is closed and the street art is left in the dark.

Literature

New York is home of the Beat Generation. They were a group of writers in the 1950s, who wrote about American culture after World War II. The most important writers of this period were Jack Kerouac, Allen Ginsberg, William S. Burroughs and Lucien Carr, who met each other while they were students at New York's Columbia University.

Do you know...?

One of Jack Kerouac's most famous books is *On The Road*. He wrote it in 1957 and it talks about his travels across America with his friends.

Comics

The American comic book was first invented in New York in the early 1930s. Many stories about superheroes used New York as their setting* such as Gotham City (Batman) and Metropolis (Superman). Marvel Comics were the first to use the real New York in their stories such as in *Spiderman* and *The Fantastic Four*.

Dreaming of New York

D

5 **In the last part of the 19th century many people in Europe and other countries saw America as a place where you could live a good life and make your dreams come true. At that time many people decided to move to America. This still happens today. Let's find out about some of the people who are living the 'American dream' in New York.**

A simple idea

Felix Sanchez de la Vega Guzman arrived in New York from Mexico more than 40 years ago. He had no money and could only speak a few words of English. His first job in New York was as a dishwasher*.

In his free time he started making tortillas, a popular Mexican food, and he sold them. People loved his tortillas and his business grew. He now has several factories across America and he's a very rich man.

From Jamaica to the Bronx

Lowell Hawthorne moved from Jamaica to New York when he was 21 years old. He also arrived with nothing but found a job and started going to college. His father in Jamaica had a baker's shop and so Lionel decided to start making Jamaican food and sell it. His first Caribbean fast food restaurant was called Golden Krust and people loved it. There are now more than 120 Golden Krust fast food restaurants across America and the pop star Rihanna often goes there.

A famous songwriter

Irving Berlin was born in Russia in 1888 and his parents decided to move him and his 8 brothers to New York to have a better life. His family was very poor and Irving started singing to make a little money. Later he started working as a singing waiter and he taught himself to play the piano. He also began writing his own songs. He became very famous. He wrote songs for more than 60 years and many of them were for Broadway shows and Hollywood films.

Anyone for ice cream?

Marinos Vourderis left Greece in the 1930s and arrived in New York with only 30 cents in his pocket. He started a building company but when one of his customers couldn't pay their bill, they left him an ice cream machine instead. So he started making ice cream and began selling it. People loved his ice creams and he started selling them in supermarkets, restaurants and food trucks. When he stopped working in 2002 he was a millionaire and was known as the 'King of Italian ices'.

From finance to fashion

In 1964 Josie Natori left the Philippines and went to America. She went to university and then found a job on Wall Street. She did very well there but wanted to start her own company and so the Natori Company was born in 1977. It sells women's fashion but also perfume and things for the home. The company sells the things they make to some very important department stores in the world.

dishwasher: a person who washes the plates and dishes in a restaurant

6 **New York is full of interesting and exciting events. Every month something amazing is happening. Let's have a look!**

St Patrick's Day Parade

It's on 17th March and it's a celebration★ of Saint Patrick from Ireland. It's the biggest Saint Patrick's Day Parade in the world. The first one happened in New York on March 17th 1762 so it's a very old event. About 150,000 people take part in the parade. They play music and walk around the streets of Manhattan. People usually wear green on this day – it's the color of Ireland.

The Fourth of July

On this day there's American Independence Day. It celebrates the Declaration of Independence from Great Britain back in 1776. One of the most famous department stores in New York, Macy's, has a firework show on Brooklyn Bridge. It's on for about 25 minutes and there are more than 40,000 fireworks★. It's amazing!

Columbus Day Parade

October 12th 1492 was the day when Christopher Columbus arrived in America. In New York there has been a parade since 1929. More than 35,000 people join the event. There are music bands and floats★ that move around the streets of Manhattan. It's the biggest celebration of Italian–American culture in the world!

Greenwich Village Halloween Parade

31st October is Halloween. In Greenwich Village in New York more than 60,000 dancers, artists, musicians and circus performers join the celebration. People wear Halloween costumes and walk through the streets of Greenwich Village at night. This event first began in 1974 thanks to a New York puppet* maker and today huge puppets are in the parade.

Thanksgiving Day Parade

The last Thursday of November in the USA is Thanksgiving Day. On this day people say thanks for the past year and celebrate together with family and friends. Since 1924 there's been a parade in New York which people watch on the streets or also on TV. There are about 8,000 dancers, cheerleaders, clowns, floats and bands in the parade.

New Year's Eve

On 31st December every year many people meet together in Times Square for the last day of the year. At 11.59 a ball, which is on the roof of a building in Times Square, drops down a pole*. It takes 60 seconds and this shows the start of the new year. About 1 million people watch the event in Times Square and enjoy themselves a lot.

Over to you

What are some of the important events in your city / country? Which is your favourite one? Why?

celebration: a special day like a birthday
fireworks: coloured lights in the sky that make a noise for celebrations

floats:

puppet:

pole: a long thin piece of metal

Films and books abou

▶7 **The city of New York is often used in films and books. Do you remember King Kong on top of the Empire State Building and X-Men on Ellis Island? Godzilla in Madison Square Gardens and Wall Street in different films? Well, here are some more for you to read about!**

Extremely Loud and Incredibly Close

This is a book by Jonathan Safran Foer which also became a film. A boy called Oskar Schell, who is 9 years old, tells the story. Oskar's dad dies in the World Trade Center on September 11th 2001. Oskar finds a key in his house inside an envelope with the name 'Black' written on it. He goes around New York and looks for information about the key. He meets a lot of different people on his journey, all with the name Black, and learns a lot of things about himself and his family.

Do you know what happened on September 11th 2001?

....

Shopaholic Takes Manhattan

This book is the second in the *Shopaholic* series and tells the story of Becky Bloomswood. She's a journalist from London and her favourite hobby is shopping. She buys many things with her credit card and has many problems with the bank. In this book she goes to work in New York and goes crazy shopping in the Big Apple.

Do you like shopping? Why? Why not?

....

find out: learn something, know about something

The Nanny Diaries

This is also a book and a film and was written by two nannies who worked in New York. They wrote about their work and the children they looked after in a funny and interesting way. When the two girls wrote the book, they were students at New York University, but they also worked for about 30 different rich families in Manhattan. After their first book, they also wrote a second one called *Nanny Returns*.

Would you like to read this book? Why? Why not?

....

The Princess Diaries

This is the story of Mia Thermopolis, who lives in Manhattan. She's a normal teenager but one day she finds out* she's also a princess and that her grandmother is the queen of a place called Genovia. She keeps a diary where she writes about friends, boyfriends, family, school. There are ten books in the series by Meg Cabot and the last one finishes when Mia becomes 18 years old. There are also two films based on the novels starring Anne Hathaway.

Would you like to be a prince/princess? Why? Why not?

....

Did you know...?

The Great Gatsby by the American author F. Scott Fitzgerald is set in the 1920s in Long Island, New York. Have you read the book?

Getting around

G

There are many different ways to visit New York – if you get tired of walking, then jump on one of the many different types of transport you can find in the city.

By subway

There are 24 subway lines that work 24 hours a day, 7 days a week, 365 days a year. During the week more than 5 million people use it to get around the city. It's very old as it was opened in 1904. If you're travelling on the subway in January, don't be surprised if you see some people that are wearing coats, but no trousers. It's *No Pants Day*. It's a kind of flash mob* that started in New York in 2002.

By boat

If you like sailing, then why not take a trip on a vintage schooner (see picture). You can sail during sunset* and get a beautiful view of Manhattan and the New York skyline full of lights. Or you can take a ride on the Staten Island ferry which takes passengers from Manhattan across to Staten Island. You get a great view of the Statue of Liberty from this big boat.

By car

If you don't want to drive around New York, then you can take a ride in a limousine with your own personal driver. He will show you all the important landmarks* and you can be like a VIP for a day. If you like classic cars then you can take a tour of the city in an Aston Martin (James Bond's car) or even a Porsche!

By air

Why not take a ride in a helicopter? You can fly over the city and get a fantastic view of important landmarks* such as the Empire State Building. The rides take 15 to 25 minutes and while you're flying, you can take some great photos above the city.

By jet ski

If you want to do something that's a lot of fun, then why not do a jet ski tour along the East River? Tours take 1–3 hours and you can ski past New York landmarks such as the Statue of Liberty, the Brooklyn Bridge and lots more.

By taxi cab

The yellow taxi cab is a symbol of New York. There are more than 10,000 taxis in the city and to get a taxi you just have to stand at the side of the road and hold your arm above your head. In 1976 there was a film called *Taxi Driver*. Robert De Niro was the star of the film and he played the part of a New York taxi driver. Some people think that it's one of the best films that was ever made.

Over to you

How do you get around your town/city?

....

What's your favourite form of transport? ....

....

Which do you think is the fastest/slowest/most exciting/most comfortable form of transport in New York? ....

....

flash mob: a group of people who suddenly get together in a public place, do an unusual activity and then go away
sunset: the time of day when the sun goes down
landmarks: buildings that are a symbol of a city

History

H

Here are some of the important dates in the history of New York. Let's take a look together!

The Lenape Indians were the first people to live in 'New York'. They were hunters, fishermen and farmers.

1524 – An Italian called Giovanni da Verazzano was the first European explorer* to arrive on this part of the Atlantic coast. He was trying to find a way to sail to Asia.

1624 – The Dutch West India Company sent 30 families to live on Nutten Island. They called this place 'New Amsterdam'.

1626 – The governor of this new colony* decided to buy the bigger Manhattan Island from the Lenape who already lived there. Only 300 people were living in the colony when they moved to Manhattan but more and more people came to live there.

1664 – The British took control of New Amsterdam and gave it a new name 'New York City'.

1760 – New York became the second largest city in America.

1775-1783 – During this period there was the Revolutionary War between Great Britain and the original 13 British colonies of America.

1776 – After being a British colony for more than 100 years, New York became independent*.

1785-1790 – New York became the first capital city of the United States. George Washington became the first President of the USA.

1792 – The New York Stock Exchange opened.

1810 – With a population of 202,589, it became the biggest city in the Western world. It was also America's most important port and after the building of the Erie Canal it became an important city for trade*.

1883 – The Brooklyn Bridge was opened and became a symbol of New York.

1886 – The Statue of Liberty was given to the city of New York as a present from France. On October 28th it was put in the New York Harbor.

1902 – New York's first skyscraper was built. It was the Flatiron Building with 21 floors.

1904 – New York's first subway line was opened.

1931 – The Empire State Building and the Chrysler Building were finished.

Can you...?

After reading the information in this book, add some more important dates to the list!

explorer: a person who travels to new places to learn something about them
colony: a group of people that go to live in another country
independent: free from the control of another person or country
trade: buying and selling between people or countries

Immigration

I

New York is a very multi-cultural* city with people coming to live there from all around the world. In some parts of the city different nationalities have their own areas such as Chinatown and Little Italy. But let's find out about when and how immigration in New York started.

Arriving in New York

When the immigrants arrived in America, they arrived at a place called Ellis Island. They had to wait in a line for many hours and were asked many questions. The people who worked at Ellis Island asked them 29 different questions such as their name, job and how much money they had. About one million immigrants arrived at Ellis Island every year but not everyone could enter the USA. Some people had to go back to their countries.

Did you know...?

The first person to pass through Ellis Island in 1892 was a girl called Annie Moore. She was 15 years old from Cork, in Ireland, and sailed with her family to America. She received a 10 dollar gold coin* as a gift from the people at Ellis Island.

Today

In 1965 Ellis Island became a part of the Statue of Liberty National Monument and in 1990 a Museum of Immigration opened inside. You can learn about the history of Ellis Island and find out what happened to some of the immigrants after they left the island.

The Titanic

On 10th April 1912 the Titanic left Southampton, in England, to sail across the Atlantic Ocean towards New York. There were 2,435 passengers on the ship and many of them wanted to go to America to start a new life. But the ship never arrived in New York. It hit an iceberg* and the ship sank*. Many people lost their lives. There are different films about the Titanic but the most famous one is probably the one with Leonardo DiCaprio and Kate Winslet.

Film

In 2013 there was also a film called *The Immigrant*. The stars were the French actress Marion Cotillard and the American actor Joaquin Phoenix. It tells the story of their new life in New York after arriving at Ellis Island.

Did you know...?

Today about 100 million Americans have someone in their family who arrived in Ellis Island from other parts of the world.

Over to you

Did anyone in your family in the past go to America to find a better life? If you don't know, try to find out! ....
....
What about in your country now? Do other nationalities move there to find a better life? ....
....

multi-cultural: with many different cultures and nationalities
coin: a piece of money

iceberg:

sank: went under the sea

Jobs

J

▶ 11 **What do children from New York want to be when they grow up? Do they want to be American footballers, firemen or doctors? Let's take a look at some of the popular and also unusual jobs that you can do in New York.**

A policeman

The New York City Police Department (NYPD) has more than 34,450 police officers working for it. People who want to work for the NYPD can choose from many different areas such as working with the police dogs, fighting drug crime, gang crime, etc. Actors often play the part of NYPD officers in TV series such as *Law & Order, CSI, 24, Brooklyn Nine-Nine* and films such as *The Amazing Spider-Man, Iron Man 2, World Trade Center, The Taking of Pelham 123.*

Over to you

Would you like to be a New York police officer? Why? Why not?

....

A taxi driver

The yellow taxi cabs in New York are a symbol of the city. There are about 51,398 taxi drivers in the city. You need a license* to become a taxi driver. If the light on top of the taxi is on, then the taxi is free, but if the light is off, you have to wait for another taxi to pass. There have been many films about New York taxi drivers. The most famous is the 1976 film *Taxi Driver*. The star of the film was Robert De Niro and it was directed by Martin Scorsese.

Over to you

Would you like to be a New York taxi driver? Why? Why not?

....

A dog walker

People in New York who are very busy with their jobs and don't have time to take their dog for a walk, often pay a professional* dog walker. The first dog walker in New York was a man called Jim Buck, who opened the Jim Buck's School for Dogs in Manhattan in 1960. He did this job for 40 years and often took 6 dogs for a walk at the same time. Now the new thing in New York is dog running. You can pay a person to take your dog for a run so your dog can keep fit, even without you!

Over to you

Would you like to be a dog walker? Why? Why not?

....

A Big Apple Greeter

The people who do this 'job' in New York are all volunteers*, so they aren't paid for what they do. But they do it because they love their city! There are about 300 greeters who take tourists on tours of their city and show them their favorite places, while telling them something unusual about the place – all for free!

Over to you

Would you like to be a Big Apple Greeter? Why? Why not?

....

Did you know...?

A 'delicatessen' (or 'deli') is a type of food shop that first opened when immigrants came from different European countries during the last century. Now they are a symbol of New York and working in a 'deli' is a popular job in New York!

license: a piece of paper which says that you can do something
professional: do something as a job and not as a hobby
volunteer: help someone or do a job without being paid

Kids

K

New York has something for all ages and here are some of the things that a child or a teenager can do in the Big Apple.

New York International Children's Film Festival

Do you like going to the movies? Then this could be for you! It's a film festival of movies for children from around the world. 100 films that children from the ages of 3-18 could like are chosen and shown in different cinemas for four weeks. Children can watch the movies, learn how to make them and meet some of the people who made them.

Brooklyn Children's Museum

Here there are 30,000 different objects from the past to look at and also living animals and insects. Some of the most popular areas are Together in the City where children learn about living, working and playing together in a multi-cultural city like New York, and 'The Pizza Parlor', where children learn how to make pizza and eat it together with their friends.

FAO Schwarz

Do you like toys? Then this is the place for you! It's the oldest toy shop in America and was opened in 1862 by the German immigrant Frederick August Otto Schwarz.

FAO Schwarz now has 40 different shops in the City. Here you can find unusual toys like teddy bears that are as tall as you and you can also choose the hair color, eye color, skin color and clothes for the doll you're buying. You can also see this famous toy shop at the cinema – it has been in many films like *The Smurfs* and *Big*.

Did you know...?

You can buy a Barbie football table in the shop for $25,000.

Kids' film locations

The film *Spider-Man* was made in many different places in the city, such as the New York Public Library, Columbia University, the Lincoln Center, City Hall and the Rockefeller Center; *Mr Popper's Penguins* is the animated film where you can see Central Park Zoo, the High Line, the Metropolitan Museum, the Flatiron Building, the Empire State Building and the Guggenheim Museum; *Home Alone 2: Lost in New York* is set* in the Plaza Hotel, Central Park and in front of the Rockefeller Center Christmas tree. What about *Night at the Museum*? Do you know where it was set? At the American Museum of Natural History!

Did you know...?

At the American Museum of National History you can spend the night there with your friends or family. And maybe the objects and animals will come to life, just like in the film!

set: make a book or film happen in a place or time

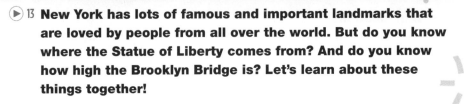

Landmarks*

L 24H LIVE

▶ 13 **New York has lots of famous and important landmarks that are loved by people from all over the world. But do you know where the Statue of Liberty comes from? And do you know how high the Brooklyn Bridge is? Let's learn about these things together!**

Statue of Liberty

When you arrive in New York it is impossible to miss this huge landmark that stands on Liberty Island. It's 46 meters high. It was designed by the French artist Bartholdi and was given to the USA as a present from the French. It's of the Roman goddess "Liberty", who is carrying a torch* in one hand and a book in the other. The date, July 4th 1776, is written on the book and this is the date of the Declaration of American Independence. In 1984 the Statue of Liberty became a UNESCO World Heritage Site and there are hundreds of copies of the statue all over the world.

Brooklyn Bridge

Another symbol of New York is this famous bridge. It's 1,825.4 meters long and people can go over the bridge by car, by bicycle or on foot. The bridge goes across the East River and joins Brooklyn to Manhattan. You can see the bridge in many films such as *Gangs of New York, I am Legend, The Dark Knight Rises, The Avengers, Godzilla.*

landmarks: monuments
torch: a small electric light that you carry in your hand
whisper: speak very quietly so not everyone can hear what you're saying

The National September 11 Memorial

This is a monument that was built to remember the 2,983 people that died in the September 11th terrorist attack on New York. It was built where the World Trade Center was before and was opened on the 10th anniversary of the attack. The names of the 2,983 people are written on the monument. In 2004, the September 11 Museum was opened to show people what happened that day and to remember the people who died.

Times Square

Times Square is near the Broadway Theatre area and is one of the world's most-visited tourist places. It is famous for its very big advertising boards. Many years ago the square was called *Longacre Square* but it changed its name in 1904 when *The New York Times* newspaper moved there. On New Year's Eve (31st December) thousands and thousands of people meet here and wait for midnight.

Grand Central Terminal

This is New York's biggest and most well-known train station. It has 67 train tracks, 44 platforms and it took 10 years to build. You can see the station and its clock in many films and TV series such as *Madagascar, Men in Black, Step Up 3, Cloverfield, The Avengers, Gossip Girl*.

Did you know...?

If you whisper* to the wall in one part of Grand Central station then the other person can hear what you're saying if they put their ear to the wall in another part of the station!

MUSICAL

Music

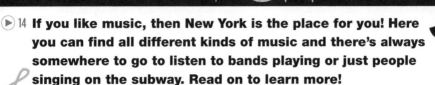

▶ 14 **If you like music, then New York is the place for you! Here you can find all different kinds of music and there's always somewhere to go to listen to bands playing or just people singing on the subway. Read on to learn more!**

The home of music

We can say that many different types of music were born in New York or have something to do with the city. For example, hip hop began in the 1970s in the Bronx before it became popular all over the world. People also say that Salsa music was born here and the style* was taken from the music of the Cuban and Puerto Rican immigrants. Other styles of music such as disco, punk rock and new wave have also been important for New York.

Where can I listen to music?

If you want to listen to classical music or a rock band or a musical, then there's always something happening. Carnegie Hall is one of the most important music halls in the world. You could also go to the Radio City Music Hall. The Lincoln Center for the Performing Arts is home to the Metropolitan Opera, New York Philharmonic, New York City Ballet, Chamber Music Society and the New York City Opera.

Did you know...?

One of the best-known composers from New York was George Gershwin. He was born in Brooklyn in 1898. He wrote songs for the Broadway theaters and some of his most famous works are *Rhapsody in Blue* and *Concerto in F.*

style: the way something is done
drops: falls down
busker: a street musician

New York, New York

One of the best-known songs about the city is *New York, New York*. It was sung in the 1977 film with the same name and Liza Minelli was the singer. In 1979 Frank Sinatra sang the song on one of his albums and since then other singers such as Beyoncé, Robbie Williams and Michael Bublé have also recorded the song. The song is played at the end of every New York Yankee game and is also used on New Year's Eve when the ball drops★ in Times Square.

Fame

Fame was an American TV series that was on TV from 1982 to 1987. It was about a group of students who went to the New York City High School for the Performing Arts. The students were all singers, musicians and dancers. It was a very popular TV series and many people were sad when the series ended.

Music on the subway

You can also listen to some good music while you're travelling on the subway. It's a popular place for 'buskers★' who play in public places to earn a little money while they're performing. Passengers in one subway station were very surprised when in May 2015 they saw the Irish band U2 'busking' at Grand Central Station!

Can you ...?

Put the words to the song *New York, New York* on each line in the right order!

a spreading news start the
b leaving today am I
c to part I it want a be of
d York New, York New

Nicknames

N

▶ 15 **Believe it or not, New York has almost 100 different nicknames. If you hear the name 'The Big Apple' or 'The City That Never Sleeps', then you know we're talking about New York. But let's read about where some of these nicknames come from.**

The Big Apple

This name was first used in the 1920s. A sports writer for a New York newspaper used the name for a horse race. Then in the 1930s black jazz musicians used the name to speak about the area of Harlem and then later on to talk about the whole city.

The City that Never Sleeps

This nickname comes from the words of the song *New York, New York*. Many shops and restaurants in New York close very late or are open 24 hours a day and so the city never goes to sleep.

The Melting Pot

In New York there are many different nationalities and groups of people of different religions and languages. This is called a "melting pot".

The City so Nice, they Named it Twice

This nickname speaks about New York as a city and New York as a state. This name was first used in *The New York Times* newspaper in 1975.

The Metropolis

This was the name of the city that was used in the Superman comics to speak about New York.

joined together: became one

The Five Boroughs

This speaks about the five different areas – the Bronx, Brooklyn, Manhattan, Queens and Staten Island – that joined together* to become New York City in 1898.

The Second City of the World

After the five boroughs of New York joined together in 1898 to become one city, New York became the second biggest city in the world after London.

The Center of the Universe

This nickname is used to speak about Times Square.

New Amsterdam

The first Dutch people to live in New York called it New Amsterdam before the British changed it to New York in 1664.

The City of Dreams

Many immigrants went to live in New York as they thought they could have a better life there.

The City of Skyscrapers

People use this nickname as New York has more skyscrapers than any other city in the world.

Over to you

Which nickname do you like the best? Why?

....

Can you think of any other good nicknames for New York?

....

Does your town/city have a nickname?

....

Outside New York

O

▶ 16 **You can spend a lot of time visiting the city of New York as there are so many things to see and do. But there are other very interesting places outside the city that are nice to see too. Let's have a look!**

Atlantic City

This is a city in New Jersey and is about 240 km from New York. It's famous for its casinos, its pier* and its beach. Its pier is very old, it opened on June 26th 1870 and was the first one in America. Atlantic City is sometimes called 'Monopoly City' because in the first Monopoly game the streets were designed like the ones in Atlantic City.

Philadelphia

This city is in Pennsylvania, about 150 km from New York. It was a very important city during the American Revolution and here the Declaration of Independence was signed* in 1776 inside Independence Hall. We can also say that America's first library, first hospital, first zoo and first stock exchange were all born in Philadelphia. You can also find the Liberty Bell in Philadelphia, the symbol of American Independence.

Did you know...?

Grace Kelly, the American actress who became the Princess of Monaco, was born in Philadelphia. Other famous people from the city are Will Smith, Ana Ortiz, who plays Hilda Suarez in the TV series *Ugly Betty*, Bradley Cooper and Taylor Kinney from *The Vampire Diaries*.

West Point

Here we can find the famous military academy. It opened in 1802 and is on the Hudson River, about 80 km from New York. Here young people go to school and study there for four years to become soldiers. In 1841 the English writer Charles Dickens visited the academy and wrote about how beautiful it was. About 65,000 students have studied at West Point among them two US Presidents, Ulysses S. Grant and Dwight D. Eisenhower.

Did you know...?

18 ex-students of the academy became NASA astronauts and 5 of them have been to the moon!

The Hamptons

This is a very rich area near New York. It's a group of villages by the sea where many rich New Yorkers have bought summer houses. The houses are some of the most expensive ones in America. Some famous people who have houses there are Jennifer Lopez, Alec Baldwin, Calvin Klein, Ralph Lauren, Steven Spielberg, Madonna and Lady Gaga. We often see or hear about this place in TV series like *Gossip Girl, Castle, Revenge, Royal Pains* and *The Real Housewives of New York*.

Over to you

Which of these places would you like to visit? Why?

....

pier: a long piece of wood that goes from the land out to sea, which you can walk on
signed: wrote your name on something to say you agree with it

43

People from New York

Ⓟ

▶ 17 **Many different kinds of people live in New York. But it's also home to some famous people too. Let's take a look at some well-known New Yorkers!**

A famous director

Who hasn't heard of Woody Allen? Well, did you know that he was born in New York and that his real name is Allan Stewart Konigsberg? He was born in the Bronx on December 1st 1935 and he is an actor, writer, film director, comedian and musician. He often plays a part in the films he writes and he's won 4 Oscars. He's directed more than 40 films such as *To Rome With Love, Magic in the Moonlight, Annie Hall, Manhattan, Hannah and her Sisters* ... and many more!

A famous singer

The American singer Christina Maria Aguilera is a New Yorker too. She was born on December 18th 1980 in Staten Island, New York. When she was a child she was in the TV series *The Mickey Mouse Club* where she sang, danced and acted. In 1999 she made her first album and her songs *Genie in a Bottle* and *What a Girl Wants* were very successful. She has now made 7 albums, won 5 Grammy Awards and sold more than 50 million records all over the world!

A famous performer*

Did you know that Lady Gaga is from New York too? She was born on March 28th 1986 in Manhattan and her real name is Stefani Joanne Angelina Germanotta. She's a singer, songwriter and actress and loves performing. She started acting in plays when she was in high school and then in 2008 she made her first album called *The Fame*, which includes songs such as *Just Dance* and *Poker Face*. She is now a great star!

44

A famous actress

Another New Yorker is the actress Scarlett Johansson. She was born on November 22nd 1984 in New York and started acting when she was very young, at 9 years old and continued* from there. In 1998 she was in the film *The Horse Whisperer* with Robert Redford and after that she became famous. Some of her many films are *Lost in Translation*, *Girl with a Pearl Earring*, *Match Point*, *The Prestige*, *The Other Boleyn Girl*, *Iron Man 2*, *The Avengers* and *Captain America*.

A famous rapper

The famous American rapper Jay Z is also from New York. His real name is Shawn Corey Carter and he was born on December 4th 1969. He's one of America's most famous rappers and has sold more than 100 million records and won 21 Grammy Awards for his music. He isn't just a rapper, but a record producer, a film producer and a businessman too.

Did you know...?

Which of these other famous Americans were born in New York?

1 ■ Robert De Niro

2 ■ Whoopi Goldberg

3 ■ Jennifer Lopez

4 ■ Paris Hilton

5 ■ Leonardo DiCaprio

performer: a person who sings in front of other people

continued: did something without stopping

Quotes

▶ 18 *The city seen from the Queensboro Bridge is always the city seen for the first time, in its first wild promise of all the mystery and beauty in the world.*
F. Scott Fitzgerald – American writer (24th September 1896-21st December 1940)

Give me such shows - give me the streets of Manhattan!
Walt Whitman - American poet and writer (31st May 1819 - 26th March 1892)

New York is the meeting place of the people, the only city where you can hardly find a typical American.
Djuna Barnes - American writer (12th June 1892 - 18th June 1982)

Make your mark in New York and you are a made man.
Mark Twain - American writer (30th November 1835 - 21st April 1910)

There is something in the New York air that makes sleep useless.
Simone de Beauvoir - French writer (9th January 1908 - 14th April 1986)

The glamour of it all! New York! America!
Charlie Chaplin - British actor and filmmaker (16th April 1889 - 25th December 1977)

One belongs to New York instantly, one belongs to it as much in five minutes as in five years.
Tom Wolfe - American writer and journalist (2nd March 1931 - present)

I go to Paris, I go to London, I go to Rome, and I always say 'There's no place like New York. It's the most exciting city in the world now. That's the way it is. That's it!
Robert De Niro - American actor - (17th August 1943 - present)

Autumn in New York, why does it seem so inviting?
Vernon Duke - Russian composer - (10th October 1903 - 16th January 1969)

One can't paint New York as it is, but rather as it is felt.
Giorgia O'Keefe - American artist - (15th November 1887 - 6th March 1986)

New York is the only real city-city.
Truman Capote - American actor and writer - (30th September 1924 - August 25th 1984)

Practically everybody in New York has half a mind to write a book - and does.
Groucho Marx - American actor and writer - (2nd October 1890 - 19th August 1977)

Over to you
Which is your favorite quote? Why?

....

....

....

Recreation

R

So how do New Yorkers spend their free time in the city? There are so many things to choose from! There are always things happening in New York – not only for the tourists but also for the people who live and work in the city!

Getting fit

People in New York love getting fit and many people spend their free time doing exercise inside or outside! New Yorkers especially love jogging and a great place to do this is Central Park. Don't be surprised if you see many mums and dads jogging while pushing their little children in their pushchairs*. This has become a new sport in the city – getting fit while spending time with your kids!

We love shopping!

In their free time New Yorkers love shopping. There are lots of different shopping areas in New York, such as Fifth Avenue, Broadway, Greenwich Village, the Meatpacking District and lots more where you can find department stores, designer clothes shops and less expensive shops. But New Yorkers love markets too. Here you can find unusual objects at a good price, often second-hand* objects or things made by hand!

Cinema

New Yorkers also enjoy going to the movies. In New York you can find all kinds of cinemas – small ones with just one screen or very big ones with many screens, old ones that were built many years ago or modern ones that show only films in 3D. And if you're feeling hungry when you're there, at some cinemas in New York you can have a meal while you're watching the movie.

Two wheels or four?

Many young people in New York love skateboarding. There are many places where it's possible to skateboard such as at the Bronx Skate Park. However, New Yorkers love skateboarding on the road too and use their skateboard as a kind of transport to get from A to B. Another activity New Yorkers love is rollerblading.

Just relaxing with friends

And of course, New Yorkers love spending time with their friends having a coffee in a bar, going for dinner together, inviting friends to their house. They love watching baseball matches and American football matches together, going for picnics when the weather is good and having a good time together!

Over to you

What do you like doing with your friends when the weather's good? And when the weather's bad?

....

pushchair:

second hand: already used, not new

49

Sport

S

▶ 20 **New Yorkers love doing and watching sport. There are sports you can do inside or outside, winter sports, summer sports... Read on to learn more!**

Baseball

One of the most popular sports to watch and play in New York is baseball. There are two baseball teams in New York – the New York Yankees and the New York Mets. In the past there were four baseball teams! The New York Giants and the Brooklyn Dodgers but they both moved to California in 1958.

American Football

Another very popular sport is American football (which is a different game from soccer). There are two main* teams in New York – the New York Giants and New York Jets. The Superbowl is the final game of the year and it's the most watched programme on TV. Michael Jackson, Madonna, Prince, The Rolling Stones, The Who and Whitney Houston have all performed here before, during and after the match.

Basketball

In New York many people watch and play basketball. The two main teams in the city are the New York Knicks and the Brooklyn Nets. There's also a team of basketball players called the Harlem Globetrotters. They don't just play basketball but they do acrobatics with the ball. They're a lot of fun to watch.

New York City Marathon

The New York City Marathon is on the first Sunday in November. People come from all over the world to do the race. Now you have to be 18 years old to run in the race but in 1977 a boy who was only 8 years old finished the race in 3 hours. He's the youngest person ever to complete the marathon. The fastest time to finish was in 2011 when a runner from Kenya finished in 2 hours and 5 minutes.

Empire State Building Run-Up

This is the world's oldest and most famous tower* race. People who do it have to run up 1,576 stairs. This usually takes 1 minute in the lift while the fastest runner usually takes 10 minutes. Do you think you could do this in 10 minutes?

Flushing Meadows

This area in New York is the city's fourth biggest park. It was built for the 1939/1940 New York World Fair. Every year the US Open Tennis Championships is played there. It's a part of the Grand Slam tennis tournaments and the others are Wimbledon, the French Open and the Australian Open.

Over to you

What's your favorite sport? Do you prefer doing sport inside or outside? Do you like going to the stadium?

....

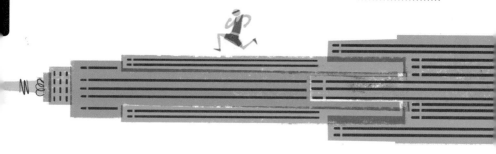

main: the most important
tower: see picture above

Theters

T

Would you like to go to the theater? Then New York is the place for you! It's full of places to see plays, comedies and musicals. There are big theaters, small theaters, old theaters and modern ones. Do you want to know more?

Broadway

This is the most important theater area in New York. It's in Manhattan and there are more than 40 theaters here. Its nickname is 'The Great White Way' as many lights are used on the theater signs to show what's on at the theater. In 2014 the theaters sold a total of $1.36 billion worth of tickets. The most popular shows to watch are musicals. Have you ever seen a musical?

The Phantom of the Opera

At the moment *The Phantom of the Opera* is the show that has been on Broadway for the longest time. It first came to New York in 1988 and is still going on. It's a musical and it was taken from a French book of the same name. It tells the story of a musician who wears a mask to cover his face and who falls in love with a beautiful opera singer.

Off-Broadway

We can say that Broadway theaters usually have more than 500 seats inside. Smaller theaters that have between 100 and 499 seats are called Off-Broadway theaters. And guess what? Theaters that are even smaller with less than 100 seats are called Off-Off Broadway!

Did you know...?

The Lyceum is the oldest operating theater on Broadway.

Anyone for a Tony?

A Tony is a special award for Broadway shows. It's similar to an Oscar for films and a Grammy for music. The awards are given every year and there are 24 different categories. The event is at the Radio City Music Hall and the record for most Tony Awards was won by the musical *The Producers* in 2001. It won 12 awards!

Unusual theaters

If you don't really like sitting in a theater and watching a play or musical, then why not try something a little different? In New York there's a theater group called 'Live In Theater' which invites people to be a part of their play. There is always a crime* and the audience* become a part of the show and play the part of a police officers and help the actors to solve* the crime.

Phantom of the Opera

Can you complete a part of the song with the missing words?

> our   you   me   of   my

Sing once again with ....
.... strange duet
.... power over you grows stronger yet
And though .... turn from me to glance behind
The phantom .... the Opera is there
Inside your mind.

crime: something very bad that someone does and for which you can go to prison
audience: people who watch or listen to a play, concert...
solve: find the answer to something

Unusual places

U

▶ 22 **Would you like to visit a different kind of place? Somewhere unusual? Something that you've never seen before? Let's have a look together!**

Staten Island Boat Graveyard

This is a very unusual place. It's the place where ships go to die! There are all kinds of boats and ships and they're taken there when they are old and not used anymore. People like taking photos and painting pictures of this strange place and a TV documentary was made about it.

The Berlin Wall

Many people think that you can only see the Berlin Wall in Germany, but this isn't one hundred percent true. You can find a small part of the wall in New York too! It's in a small square at 520 Madison Avenue and it's been there since 1990 just after the Berlin Wall came down. On it you can see artwork by two artists – Thierry Noir and Kiddy Citny.

Pneumatic tubes

These were 'tubes' that were used to move different things around the city and from place to place. For example, they were used to send post around the city and they were used to move garbage*.
They were also used in the New York Public Library to send books from one floor to another. You can still see them now in some parts of the city.

garbage: things that you don't want any more

The world's largest chess board

If you go to 767 Third Avenue, you'll find something surprising on the wall of the building – a huge chess board. The chess pieces are moved only once a week on a Wednesday, so one game can take a very long time! Near the board there's a sign that says "Can you guess who will win?"

Did you know...?

New York's oldest magic shop is Tannen's Magic Shop. It was opened in 1925 by Louis Tannen and there is also the Tannen's Magic School and a summer camp for young magicians.

A restaurant on a train

If you go to the top floor of Bloomingdale's department store, don't be surprised if you find a train that looks very old but doesn't move. This is a restaurant called *Le Train Bleu* and was built like the *Calais-Mediterranée Express*, a train that went from Calais, in the north of France, to the French Riviera from 1886 to 2007. The writer Agatha Christie wrote about the train in one of her books *The Mystery of the Blue Train*.

Track 61

This is a secret subway station that was used especially by President Franklin D. Roosevelt to move from Grand Central Station to the Waldorf Astoria Hotel without people seeing him. Other famous people have used it too. It was also used in the film *The Amazing Spider-Man 2*.

Over to you

Which place do you think is the most interesting to visit?

....

Do you have any unusual places in your city / country?

....

Views of New York

V

▶ 23 **Where's the best place to get a wonderful view of New York? From the top of the Statue of Liberty? From the Empire State Building or the Brooklyn Bridge? Yes, but not only! Come with us to find more great views of the city!**

Governors' Island

This is a small island in the Bay of New York and is just 732 meters from Manhattan. It's a great place for cycling or having a picnic, but it's only open from May to September. There has been the 'World Trade Center Run to Remember' there since 2009, on the first Sunday of September every year.

One World Observatory

It was opened on May 29th 2015 and is at the top of the One World Trade Center. You can get great views from the 100th, 101st and 102and floors and you can walk around to see different places. How long does it take to arrive at the top? In the lift just 47 seconds! As you go up in the very fast lift, you can see pictures of views of New York from the 1600s to today.

Roosevelt Island Tramway

This is a kind of tram that isn't on the ground, but in the air! It goes across the East River and joins Roosevelt Island to Manhattan. Each 'cabin' holds 110 people and there are 115 trips every day. It climbs up to 76 meters and from there you can get wonderful views of Manhattan. You can see the tram in many films and TV series set in New York such as *Spiderman* and *CSI New York*. We can also see a virtual Roosevelt Island tram in the video game series *Grand Theft Auto*.

30 Rockefeller Center

This very tall skyscraper in New York has many different nicknames such as 30 Rock and The Slab. It's 259 meters tall, has 70 floors and inside there are the offices of the NBC, the American TV and radio station. It was built in 1933 and you can get to the final floor of the building, called Top of the Rock, and see a wonderful view of the city. There's a famous photo that was taken while they were building the skyscraper. Some workers are sitting high up, taking a break and having their lunch. It was taken on September 20th 1932.

Did you know...?

Why not join together culture and great views? On top of the Metropolitan Museum there's a lovely roof garden where you can see Central Park and Manhattan. You can also eat and drink something there while you are looking at the artwork on the roof with the city of New York in front of you.

Over to you

Where are the best views in your city/country?

....

Wall Street
W

▶ 24 **Wall Street is only 1.1 km long but it's one of the most famous streets in New York. It's the financial center of the city and is in Manhattan. Let's learn more!**

Its history

In the past, Wall Street was called De Waal Straat. It was given this name by Dutch people who lived in the city. People think that they used this name as they built a wall there to keep themselves safe from the native Americans.

In the 18th century, it became a place of finance as a group of 24 people agreed to buy and sell their goods* with each other and the New York Stock Exchange was born.

A black period

The 1920s was a very good period for the USA. Many people were rich and wanted to make money. They did business on the Stock Exchange and only thought about money. But in 1929 everything went wrong and people lost all their money. This period is called the Wall Street Crash or Black Tuesday. This was the start of The Great Depression, a very hard time that continued for 10 years.

Did you know...?

Every morning at 9.30 at the New York Stock Exchange somebody rings a bell for the start of business. At 4pm somebody rings the bell again for the end of the working day. Very often a famous or important person comes to ring the bell.

goods: things you can buy and sell
honest: a good person, someone who doesn't do bad things and doesn't lie
prison:

Wall Street - the films

There are many films that speak about Wall Street. The first one was made in 1987 by the American film director Oliver Stone. It was called *Wall Street* and the actors in the film were Michael Douglas and Charlie Sheen. It was about a man called Gordon Gekko who worked in finance but wasn't a very honest* man. In 2010 there was the second film of the series and it was called *Wall Street: Money Never Sleeps*. The same actors were in the film but this time Gordon Gekko is a different man and tries to be an honest and good person.

The Wolf of Wall Street

Another film that speaks about Wall Street was in the cinema in 2013. The star was Leonardo DiCaprio and the film tells the story of Jordan Belfort. He worked in finance during the 1990s and he wrote a book about his life. He did many wrong things in his work and went to prison* for twenty-two months.

Not only work

Many tourists visit Wall Street when they come to New York. They enjoy visiting the famous landmarks in the area like Trinity Church, the Federal Reserve (it has $100 billion of gold which is kept in a safe place) and the New York Stock Exchange.

Did you know...?

On April 30th 1789 George Washington became the first president of the USA. This happened at Federal Hall on Wall Street.

Xmas

X

25

Christmas is a wonderful time of year in any place, but especially in New York! There's so much to see and do and the city becomes a place of magic. Read on to learn more!

Pop-up Christmas markets

At this time of year, New York is full of Christmas markets. One of these is the Winter Solstice and Holiday Market at Queens Botanical Gardens. Here you can enjoy the lovely gardens while shopping for gifts, and children can listen to stories and make Christmas cards and presents. You can find another Christmas market in Central Park as well as in lots of other places in the city.

Turning on the lights

Christmas isn't Christmas without a huge tree and you can find lots of these in New York. The biggest and most famous one is at the Rockefeller Center whose 30,000 Christmas lights are turned on at the beginning of December. Every year this event is watched by thousands of happy, excited people. After September 11th 2001, many people from around the world came to see the tree with red, blue and white lights like the American flag.

Do you know...?

Don't be surprised if you see hundreds and hundreds of Santa Claus running towards you in New York. This is SantaCon, a Christmas party that happens on the streets of New York every year. People have to wear the same clothes as Santa Claus and have fun. This also happens in many other cities around the world but the one in New York is the biggest. Last year about 30,000 people were there!

Christmas ice-skating

During the winter months, in New York it's possible to go ice-skating in many different places. You can do this in Central Park, Rockefeller Center and Bryan Park. You can choose to go skating during the day while looking at a wonderful view of the city or at night with all the lights of the buildings and Christmas lights.

Singing at Christmas

If you like singing, then you could go 'caroling' in New York at Christmas. A carol is a Christmas song that is sung in church or by groups of singers in the street. Popular carols are *Silent Night, Jingle Bells, oh Christmas Tree* and many more.

Swimming with polar bears

Well, not quite! But there's a club in New York called the Coney Island Polar Bear Club who swim in the ocean near Coney Island during the winter months! The water is freezing* but this isn't a problem for them! Every New Year's Day they go for a swim to celebrate the New Year and lose a few kilos after eating a lot at Christmas!

Would you like to try this?

freezing: very, very cold

Yummy things to eat

Y

26

Are you feeling hungry? Yes? Well, you can find all kinds of things to eat in New York. Let's have a look at some of the amazing and unusual places and things you can eat.

Singing while you eat

This is a restaurant which is all about the 1950s in the theater area of Broadway. The waiters and waitresses who work there sing while they're serving you. It's called Ellen's Stardust Diner and inside you can find many objects from the 1950s. There's a TV from 1956 and a cinema screen that shows films from the 1950s.

Dr Jekyll and Mr Hyde

Have you read the book *Dr Jekyll and Mr Hyde* by the Scottish writer Robert Louis Stevenson? This restaurant and bar in Manhattan has the same 'horror' theme as the book. While you eat, there are actors who play a part and wear different clothes. You can also hear strange sounds and there are special effects*. Are you afraid?

Lots of peanut butter

If you like peanut butter, then you'll love this place. It's a sandwich shop in Greenwich Village and only sells things made from peanut butter. Yum, yum!

Take your dog

Would you like to visit a restaurant where many of the customers are dogs? Then this is the place for you! The Barking Dog serves normal food and drink but if you take your dog with you, then there's something for your dog to eat and drink too.

In 1871 a butcher from Germany started selling hot dog in Coney Island in New York. Since then they have become a symbol of New York. You have to eat them with a lot of onions, ketchup and mustard on top!

The Cronut

Do you know what it is? It's a kind of croissant and doughnut together and it was first made by chef Dominique Ansel in New York in 2013. In December 2013 *Time* magazine called the Cronut one of the best inventions* of 2013. New Yorkers love the Cronut!

Food trucks

These are small trucks* that move around the city selling street food. They can move from place to place around the city. You need a license to sell food from one of these trucks and you can eat all kinds of food from the usual pizza, hot dogs and sandwiches to the food of different countries such as Taiwanese, Greek, French, Arabic and Spanish.

Every year on 4th July, American Independence Day, there's Nathan's Famous Hot Dog Eating competition. The winner is the person who eats the most hot dogs in 10 minutes. For the last 8 years the same person has won the competition. In 2014 he ate 61 hot dogs in 10 minutes! How many could you eat in 10 minutes?

Over to you

What's your favorite food? Do you have any unusual restaurants in your city / country? ......

special effects: scenes in a film made by computer to make it more exciting
inventions: things that are made for the very first time

truck:

Zoos and parks

Z

▶ 27 **Maybe you'll be surprised to hear this, but New York is a very green city. There are more than 1,700 parks and 14% of the city is green. People use these green areas to relax and to do sport. Let's learn more!**

Central Park

This is the biggest and most famous park in New York. In 1962 it became a National Historic Landmark and about 37.5 million people visit the park every year. So what can you do there? Anything you want! There are green areas for doing sport or just relaxing. There are several lakes as well as two places to do ice-skating, one of which becomes a swimming pool in the summer. There is also an outside theater where it's possible to watch some of Shakespeare's plays in the summer months. The park even has its own police station inside!

Do you know...?

A part of the park is a monument to John Lennon. After he died, many different countries sent trees to the park and they built an area called 'Strawberry Fields' to remember him.

Central Park Zoo

Inside the park there's also a zoo. It's quite a small zoo and has been there since the 1860s. You can see it in many different films such as the animated film *Madagascar*, *The Wild* and *Mr Popper's Penguins*.

Bronx Zoo

This is one of the biggest zoos in the world. Inside there are about 6,000 animals and 650 different species. So what do people like most about the zoo? Well, visitors love the Congo Gorilla Forest and the *Wild* Asia

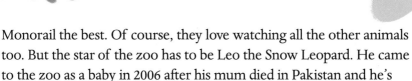

Monorail the best. Of course, they love watching all the other animals too. But the star of the zoo has to be Leo the Snow Leopard. He came to the zoo as a baby in 2006 after his mum died in Pakistan and he's lived in the zoo since then. His story was made into a book.

A very clever elephant!

In 1914 some words were found on the wall of the elephant house in the Bronx zoo. Everyone in the zoo said they didn't write them so some people believed that Gunda the elephant wrote them! What do you think?

Did you know...?

In 1916, the Bronx Zoo built the world's first animal hospital inside the zoo.

The High Line

It's a very popular green area in New York. It was a train track that isn't used anymore and was built above the ground. There you can see lots of different wild plants and some interesting art and architecture.

Gardens on the roof

New York also has a lot of 'secret' gardens that you can't see from the street. You have to look up to the sky as many of them are on top of the buildings! Many bars, hotels and restaurants have roof gardens but also many private homes have one too! So don't look down but look up!

Over to you

Do you like animals? What's your favorite animal?

....

Activity pages

1

1 How many boroughs are there in New York?
2 Which building in New York is the fourth tallest in the world?
3 Which museum of art opened in 1870 and is near Central Park?
4 What's the 'American Dream'?
5 What happens on the last Thursday of November in the USA?
6 What happens in the book *Extremely Loud and Incredibly Close*?
7 Can you remember five different ways to get around New York?
8 When did New Amsterdam become New York?
9 Who was the first person to pass through Ellis Island in 1892?
10 Can you name some jobs that New Yorkers do?
11 If you want to buy a teddy bear, a doll and a toy car which famous shop can you go to?
12 What's the name of New York's biggest train station?
13 Who was George Gershwin?
14 Do you remember five different nicknames for New York?
15 Why is Philadelphia an important city?
16 Which famous people were born in New York?
17 Can you remember any of the quotes about New York?
18 What are some of the things you can do in New York in your free time?
19 Who are the New York Yankees and the New York Mets?
20 What's Broadway famous for?
21 What can you find at 767 Third Avenue?
22 Can you name three places where you can get great views of New York?
23 What happens every morning at 9.30 at the New York Stock Exchange?
24 Where can you find the biggest Christmas tree in New York?
25 What did a German butcher start selling in Coney island in 1871?
26 Where can you find 6,000 animals in New York?

Wordsearch

2 Can you find fifteen words about New York in the word search?

```
D B U I L D I N G S B
O S U B W A Y C I T Y
W I X B M U S I C A L
N S K Y S C R A P E R
T L M U S E U M T O P
O A M O N E Y L I F E
W N E W S P A P E R S
N D I A R Y S T O R Y
I M M I G R A T I O N
```

Writing

3 Send your friends a postcard from New York. Tell them about the city, what you're doing and what you've seen! (write about 50 words).

Listening ▶ 2

4 **Listen to the text about Areas in New York and put True or False.**

		T	F
1	About 9.4 million people live in New York.	○	○
2	In New York there are five areas that are called 'boroughs'.	○	○
3	In Queens there was the World Fair in 1949.	○	○
4	In the Yankee Stadium in the Bronx you can watch baseball matches.	○	○
5	The American writer Edgar Allan Poe lived in the Bronx in 1846.	○	○
6	The boxer Mike Tyson and the basketball player Michael Jordan were born in the Bronx.	○	○
7	You can only get to Staten Island by taking a boat.	○	○
8	Many tourists visit Manhattan.	○	○

Adjectives

5 **Put the right adjective about New York in the sentences.**

> rich   tall   popular   amazing   expensive   famous

1 The views from the top of the Empire State Building are _____.

2 Many _____ people such as Woody Allen and Lady Gaga come from New York.

3 In New York there are many_____ buildings. These are called skyscrapers.

4 Some of the most _____ places to visit in New York are Central Park, Times Square and the Statue of Liberty.

5 The Hamptons is a _____ area where you can find some very _____ houses.

Find the word

6 **Read the definitions and find the right word!**

1 Important things to see in a city/country. _____

2 An informal name that someone gives you. _____

3 A very tall building. _____

4 The time and place of a film/book. _____

5 A special day like a birthday. _____

6 Buildings that are a symbol of a city. _____

7 With many different cultures and nationalities. _____

8 A prize. _____

9 People who watch or listen to a play or concert. _____

10 Scenes in a film made by computer to make it more exciting.

_____

Places in the snake

7 **Can you divide the snake into the different places to visit in New York? How many different words can you make out of the snake? e.g. _book, tree_... Make at least 20!**

STATUEOFLIBERTYBROOKLYNBRIDGEEMPIRESTATEBUILDINGWALLSTREETFLATIRONBUILDINGONEWORLDTRADECENTERTIMESSQUAREBROADWAY

Fill in the gaps

8 **Read the summary about this very popular park and fill in the gaps.**

> sport   biggest   opened   has   famous   areas   park

This is the **(1)** _____ and most **(2)** _____ park in New York. It **(3)** _____ in 1857 and is 341 hectares. There are green **(4)** _____ for doing **(5)** _____ or just relaxing. The **(6)** _____ even **(7)** _____ its own police station inside!

What's the name of this park? _____

Speaking

9 **Talk to your classmates about these questions!**

1 Have you ever visited New York?

NO   Would you like to go there? Why? Why not?

YES   When did you go there?
   Who did you go with?
   Did you like it?
   What did you see there?
   How long did you spend there?
   Would you like to go back?

2 Why is New York so popular with tourists?

3 What do you think is the most exciting thing to do in New York?

Matching

10 **Can you match these famous New York landmarks with their description?**

1 ◯ Wall Street
2 ◯ Brooklyn Bridge
3 ◯ One World Observatory
4 ◯ The Metropolitan Museum of Art
5 ◯ Empire State Building

a It's on Fifth Avenue and has 102 floors.
b It's near Central Park and is one of the world's biggest and most important art museums.
c It's a very small area but a very rich one!
d It was opened in May 2015 and from the top you can 'see forever'.
e It was built in 1834 and is 1,825 meters long. You can go across it by car, by bicycle or on foot.

11 **Look at one of the photos on the following pages and describe it. Talk about what you can see in the photo and what's happening. Don't tell your classmates which picture you're describing. They have to guess!**

12 **Choose one of the topics from the book, for example Areas in New York and tell your classmates what you remember. Try to talk for 2 minutes!**

Teen (ELI) Readers

Stage 1
Maureen Simpson, *In Search of a Missing Friend*
Charles Dickens, *Oliver Twist*
Geoffrey Chaucer, *The Canterbury Tales*
Janet Borsbey & Ruth Swan, *The Boat Race Mystery*
Lucy Maud Montgomery, *Anne of Green Gables*
Mark Twain, *A Connecticut Yankee in King Arthur's Court*
Mark Twain, *The Adventures of Huckleberry Finn*
Angela Tomkinson, *Great Friends!*
Edith Nesbit, *The Railway Children*
Eleanor H. Porter, *Pollyanna*
Anna Sewell, *Black Beauty*
Kenneth Grahame, *The Wind in the Willows*

Stage 2
Elizabeth Ferretti, *Dear Diary...*
Angela Tomkinson, *Loving London*
Mark Twain, *The Adventures of Tom Sawyer*
Mary Flagan, *The Egyptian Souvenir*
Maria Luisa Banfi, *A Faraway World*
Frances Hodgson Burnett, *The Secret Garden*
Robert Louis Stevenson, *Treasure Island*
Elizabeth Ferretti, *Adventure at Haydon Point*
William Shakespeare, *The Tempest*
Angela Tomkinson, *Enjoy New York*
Frances Hodgson Burnett, *Little Lord Fauntleroy*
Michael Lacey Freeman, *Egghead*
Michael Lacey Freeman, *Dot to Dot*
Silvana Sardi, *The Boy with the Red Balloon*
Silvana Sardi, *Scotland is Magic!*
Silvana Sardi, *Garpur: My Iceland*
Silvana Sardi, *Follow your Dreams*
Gabriele Rebagliati, *Naoko: my Japan*

Stage 3
Anna Claudia Ramos, *Expedition Brazil*
Charles Dickens, *David Copperfield*
Mary Flagan, *Val's Diary*
Maureen Simpson, *Destination Karminia*
Anonymous, *Robin Hood*
Jack London, *The Call of the Wild*
Louisa May Alcott, *Little Women*
Gordon Gamlin, *Allan: My Vancouver*